A TEMPLAR BOOK

First published in the UK in 2016 by Templar Publishing.
This edition published in the UK in 2017 by Templar Publishing,
an imprint of Kings Road Publishing, part of the Bonnier Publishing Group,
The Plaza, 535 King's Road, London, SW10 0SZ
www.templarco.co.uk
www.bonnierpublishing.com

ISBN 978-1-78370-848-2

Illustrated by Daron Parton
Written by Emma Dodson & Tasha Percy
Designed by Kieran Hood and Mark Mckinley
Edited by Eryl Nash and Tasha Percy

Printed in China

templar
books

THE REALLY Gross ANIMALS BOOK

Emma Dodson & Daron Parton

ANIMALS ARE GROSS!

ROTTEN BOTTOM
Who knew that poop and farts could be so useful in the animal kingdom? Find out how bum power is used in the wild.

BUGS, BITES AND PARASITES
Ever heard of a vampire louse? These miniature monsters can do some disgusting damage!

EXPLODING TOADS
Find out what caused these toads to blow in this strange mystery...

ROTTEN REPTILES AND FREAKY FROGS
Which slobbery reptile could kill you with its deadly drool? And which can slip out of its skin in one go?

STAY COOL!
Animals have some gross ways of controlling their body temperature, such as peeing on their legs and dancing on poo...

FUNKY FISH
Underwater animals can be really disgusting. Ever heard of the black swallower?

BOTTOMS UP

Did you know that the average burping and farting cow can make as much greenhouse gas as a family car in just one year?

BAD TABLE MANNERS

We all have bad habits but some animals have some terrifying table manners.

I LOVE EEEUUW

The animal kingdom is full of gruesome rituals, such as blowing your nostrils into a balloon and exchanging gifts of pee and puke!

DISGUSTING DEFENCES

Some creative creatures have ingeniously icky ways of escaping their predators. Guess what happens when you frighten a hairy frog?

DEADLY SERIOUS

Can you believe that a type of ant would rather explode than be eaten? Some animals have some seriously diehard ways to avoid being eaten...

Rotten Bottoms

Many animals take an icky interest in each other's bums. Pet dogs love to smell other dog's backside to say 'hello'! Here are some more disgusting things animals do with their bums…

FANTASTIC FARTS

Manatees live in the sea and travel by farting. When it wants to sink to the bottom, a manatee lets loose a ferocious fart. But when it needs to get back to the surface, the manatee holds its farts in – so that all the gas turns its belly into a big balloon and it floats back up to the top.

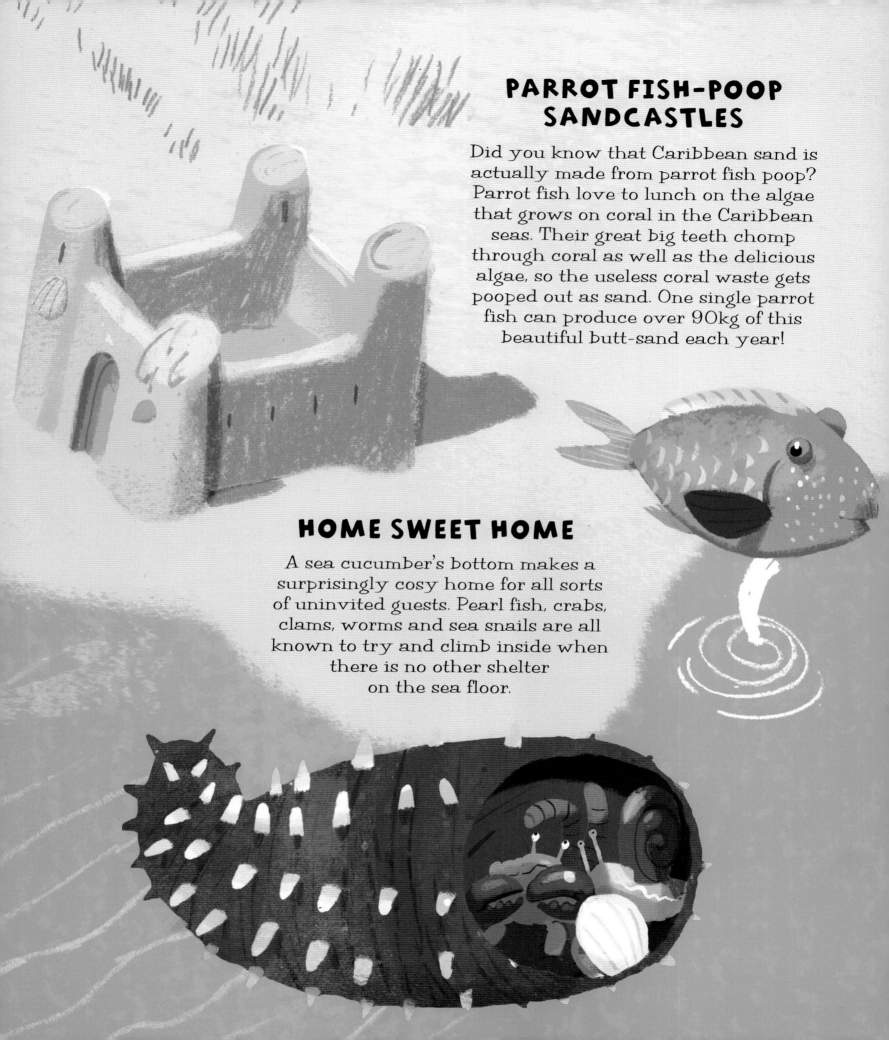

PARROT FISH-POOP SANDCASTLES

Did you know that Caribbean sand is actually made from parrot fish poop? Parrot fish love to lunch on the algae that grows on coral in the Caribbean seas. Their great big teeth chomp through coral as well as the delicious algae, so the useless coral waste gets pooped out as sand. One single parrot fish can produce over 90kg of this beautiful butt-sand each year!

HOME SWEET HOME

A sea cucumber's bottom makes a surprisingly cosy home for all sorts of uninvited guests. Pearl fish, crabs, clams, worms and sea snails are all known to try and climb inside when there is no other shelter on the sea floor.

Bottoms Up

Food that comes out of animals bums can have many different uses. For some animals, it can be eaten again. Sometimes humans use it, for making cars go or for a tasty treat...

THE POWER OF THE FART

Cows burp and fart so much that they harm our planet with the amount of methane, a harmful gas, they produce. There's even a bus in England that is solely powered by the methane release from cow manure and farts!

SNACK TIME!

Rabbits have two types of poo: little hard, round balls that drop out of their bums and dark, smelly ones that they suck into their mouths to eat! These nutritious snacks are called cecals and are an essential part of a healthy rabbit's diet.

MUM'S BUM IS YUM!

Koalas eat eucalyptus leaves, which are hard to digest and often poisonous. Young koalas need special bacteria in their guts to digest the leaves. But the only way to get this bacteria is to lick it out of their mums' bums!

TASTY BEAVER BOTTOM

Have you eaten any beaver bottom today? You may not think so, but if you've eaten vanilla, strawberry or raspberry ice cream, you may have come closer to a beaver's bottom than you think! Some natural flavourings used in ice cream, yoghurts and sweets have been made from a slimy-brown substance called castoreum, which is produced in a beaver's bum.

MR. BEAVER'S ~~BOTTOM~~ ICE CREAM

Now with Beaver's Secret Special Ingredient!

Bad Table Manners

Some animals eat gross things. Poop, pee, vomit… They all make delicious dishes. But watch out — some animals might also try to share their disgusting dinners with you!

POOP Á LA CARTE

A housefly's favourite food is poo, but it's also happy to share your lunch! Houseflies taste through their feet, so as soon as one starts walking on your cheese sandwich, it's dropping poop. The fly will then vomit on your sandwich – throwing up a delicious soup of saliva and half-digested food – before sucking it back up again with its straw-shaped tongue!

BOGEY-LICIOUS!

Did you know that the tongue of a giraffe can stretch up to 50cm in length? This super-sized tongue is great for eating up those spiky tree-top leaves. It also makes a brilliant bogie picker!

DOWN IN ONE

Snakes can eat a lot including cats, pigs, crocodiles or even an adult antelope – which can weigh up to 22.7kg. Snakes' jaws are super-stretchy so the snake can swallow its lunch in one go...

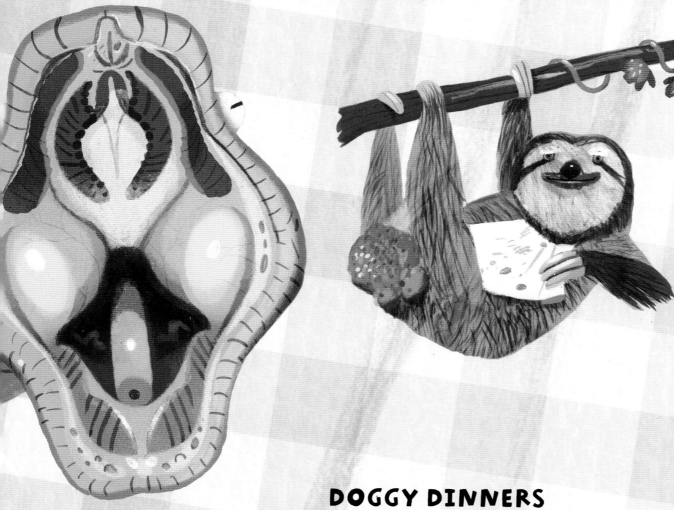

SLOTH-Y SNACKS

Sloths live in trees. But once a week, they leave their tree to have a poo. Some poo gets stuck to their bum, where moths lay their eggs. Fully-grown moths fly out of the poop and into the sloth's fur, where they die. This creates a gloopy-green algae on the sloth's fur, which the sloth loves to eat!

DOGGY DINNERS

African wild dogs make disgusting dinner guests. 'Anyone for seconds?' takes on a whole new meaning for these revolting recyclers. They will vomit up meals to share with ALL their friends and family!

I Love Eeeuuw

Some animals will dance, sing or fluff up their feathers to impress a potential mate. But a few animals have some seriously sick ways of finding love…

DANGEROUS DATING

To mate with a female, the male black widow spider has to position himself very near to the female's fangs. But if he doesn't run away as soon as they finish mating, the male spider could get eaten by his girlfriend!

BUBBLEGUM NOSE

When trying to attract a mate, the male hooded seal blows his pink nostrils inside out to create a bubblegum-like balloon, almost the size of his head! Just in case the girl hasn't noticed, he bounces his bubble about until she falls in love with him.

BUBBLEGUM

PRICKLY PORCUPINES

A male porcupine tempts his potential porcupine princess with a special gift, to avoid getting stabbed on her spiky quills – he completely covers her in wee! If she likes him she exposes her soft, non-prickly underbelly so that the male can approach her... without getting poked.

LOVE SICK

To show his affection, a male white-fronted parrot waits until he is kissing a female, before vomiting straight into her mouth.

HIPPOCOPTER

Male hippos protect their territories and show off to the ladies by weeing, pooing and spinning their tails at the same time – spraying all their mucky mixture through the air!

Disgusting Defences

Running, hiding, distraction and disguise are popular tactics used by animals to avoid their predators but they also have some disgusting secret weapons!

A GECKO'S TAIL

If a lizard or gecko is caught by its back-end, it can simply run away, leaving its tail with its confused attacker. Amazingly the tail keeps wriggling while the lizard makes a dash for it...

BEETLE JUICE

When the bombardier beetle is under attack, it points its bum at the attacker and squirts chemicals out of its bottom. They create a boiling toxic goo that burns its predator!

TERRIFYING TORPEDOS

The Texas horned lizard has a special way of scaring off attackers. It increases the blood pressure in a pouch below its eyes till the blood shoots out.

It can fire this torpedo of blood one whole metre!

TOXIC ELBOWS

The slow loris stops itself from being eaten by licking poisonous pads on its elbows, then drooling the venom all over the rest of its body. This stops its enemies taking a bite. All this licking also gives it a pretty poisonous mouth... so predators need to beware that it doesn't bite back!

X-MEN FROGS

When a hairy frog is under attack, it will break its own toe bones and shoot them out of its skin like cat's claws, to scare away its enemy.

Deadly Serious

When threatened or attacked some animals will do anything to avoid being eaten, from making themselves explode to faking death!

EXPLODING ANTS

Ever had your food explode in your face? This can happen if you're an anteater who fancies some Malaysian ants for supper. When the ant feels threatened, it squeezes the muscles in its abdomen and explodes, splattering poison and bits of its body all over its enemy.

KABOOM!

PLAYING DEAD

The opossum will hiss, growl and bite to stop predators. But when that doesn't work it will fall to the ground and foam at the mouth, as if it has dropped dead from a disgusting disease. It will also produce a stinky green substance from its bum that smells like a decaying animal...

STINKY SKUNKS

The stinky liquid that a skunk squirts out of its bum can temporarily blind a predator.

Funky Fish

Some of the strangest, most terrifying creatures live at the bottom of the sea. They survive in total darkness at depths where the water pressure would crush a human!

SLIME ATTACK

Hagfish are slippery, sausage-shaped fish that live at the bottom of the sea. They have hundreds of slime pores running along their bodies, so if they're bitten by a big fish, they shoot expanding gloop that chokes and suffocates their predator.

GO LARGE

The black swallower is a small fish with a big appetite! It can happily swallow a fish twice its own length. But if it isn't careful, its big appetite can be the death of it... If a meal doesn't get digested before it rots, it releases gasses inside the swallower's belly, making it float up to the surface of the sea and die!

BUBBLE-BLOWING BEAUTIES

The deep, dark oceans around Australia are home to some truly ugly fish...

Blobfish look like grumpy lumps of jelly. They're gentle, slow-moving creatures that bob about quietly in the deep ocean, eating little crabs and anything edible that floats into their mouths.

The ogrefish (nicknamed 'fangtooth') looks very creepy. This monster has teeth so big it can't close its mouth. However, it's very small and almost totally blind.

The Really Gross Animals' FREAKSHOW

BLOBFISH

OGREFISH

Stay Cool!

When it gets hot, animals that can't sweat have to find other ways to cool down. While elephants, hippos, rhinos and pigs cool off by rolling in mud, other animals have equally stinky ways to stop themselves burning up...

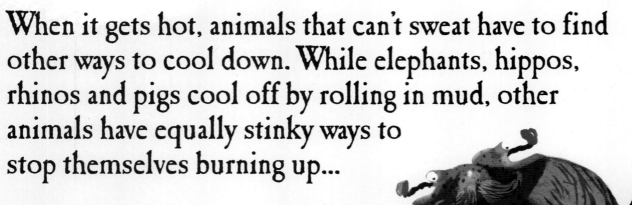

KEEP COOL, DANCE ON POO

Dung beetles spend most of their days rolling huge balls of poop around on hot sand. To prevent their feet from burning dung beetles use their poop balls to cool down. There's moisture in a dung ball, so when a beetle gets too hot, it hops up on top to cool down.

PANT AND DROOL

Dogs have a big fur coat (and love chasing sticks on hot, sunny days), so can get very hot. By hanging its tongue out and panting, a dog gets hot breath out and cool air in. When the cool air hits its wet tongue, it lowers its body temperature. Now that's some clever drool!

PEE PANTS

The turkey vulture is a dirty bird, peeing on its legs to stop it from getting too hot! It's called urohydrosis and works because the wee evaporates off the skin, cooling the vulture's legs in the process. The acid in their wee also kills the bacteria on their feet, which they get from standing on rotten flesh...

WEE-DRINKING FROGS

Frogs need water and will die if they get too hot. Water-holding frogs live in hot, dry parts of Australia but these clever creatures have a handy water storage system in their bladder – so they can cool down with a nice drink of pee!

Water-holding frogs also have big, flipper-like feet that make good shovels. When it gets too hot, the frog digs a deep hole in the sand, uses the slimy mucus from its skin to make a watertight coat for itself, and climbs into its hole with a bladder full of water. Then it'll stay like that until the rainy season.

Rotten Reptiles and Freaky Frogs

Reptiles and amphibians have some pretty strange habits, from how they look after their young to how they protect themselves from danger.

BABY DADDY

Darwin's frogs have a strange way of giving birth. The females lay the eggs but as soon as they hatch into tadpoles, the males swallow them. Up to 19 tadpoles can swim around inside the male. Then, after six weeks, they hop out of his mouth as fully-formed frogs!

BRUTAL NEWT

If a Spanish ribbed newt is attacked, it shoots its ribs out through its skin, creating spiky spears along both sides of its body. The newt also produces a poisonous, milky liquid from its skin... enough to put any predator off its lunch.

BIN THE SKIN

All animals (even humans) shed their skin, bit-by-bit, as they grow. The skin of a snake is not stretchy, so when it grows too big, it simply slides out of its tight, old skin in one go – as if it is taking off a dirty, worn-out sock! This process leaves the snake with soft, shiny skin.

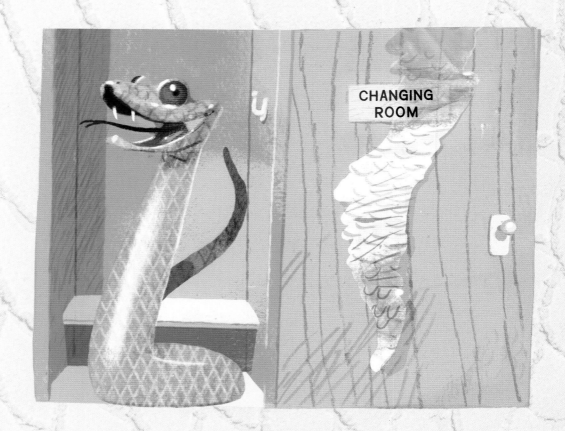

TWO-HEADED TERROR

Snakes are one of the most common animals to be born with two heads and usually have very short lives. Moving can be tricky, with the two brains disagreeing on which direction is best, and fights for food can end in disaster!

DEADLY DRIBBLE

The Komodo dragon is a very large lizard. A single bite from this beast will kill you – not because of its sharp teeth, but because of its deadly dribble! The Komodo dragon's mouth is full of poisonous dribble that slowly kills its prey.

Exploding Toads

In April 2005, a gruesome mystery confused scientists in Hamburg, Germany: a small pond became the scene of approximately 1,000 unexplained toad deaths. These were no ordinary deaths – the toads had been seen swelling up to over three times their body size before exploding! Find out more here...

Operation: Guts and Gizzards		Date: 24th Oct 2005
Investigator: PC Frogman	**Location:** Small pond in east Hamburg.	
Victims:	approx. 1,000 common European toads.	
Crime scene description:	Large numbers of toads appear to have swollen up and exploded. Guts were found up to 1 metre away from each exploded toad. See exhibits A and B.	
Initial analysis:	Tests have been made for possible causes of the deaths. Results proved negative for all likely viruses and fungal infections. Needs further investigation.	

Exhibit A

Trajectory of toad gizzards

1 metre

Pond

Exhibit B

Photo of exploded toad at location

Diagram 1
Location of
toad liver.

Diagram 2
Crow attacks
toad, takes liver.
Toad swells up.

Diagram 3
Toad explodes.

G S I

Gross Scene Investigation

SOLVED

The mystery of the exploding toads

Case No: 0276/41178

Operation: Guts and Gizzards

Location: East Hamburg

Statement

Further examinations were made of dead
and living toads.

All exploded toads have a small, circular cut
on their back, about the same size as a crow's
beak. No toad livers could be found at the
scene of the explosions.

Conclusion: A toad's skin is poisonous to
crows. The liver is the only part that a crow
enjoys eating. Cunning crows learned to make
a hole in the skin of a toad and pull out its
liver. The toad naturally puffs up in defence
but, without a liver to hold its internal organs
inside, its lungs stretch until they burst –
scattering organs all over the place.

Status:

CASE
SOLVED

Signed:

Name: Dr Frank Mutschmann

Bugs, Bites and Parasites

Parasites are sneaky little creatures that hide on or inside animals (including humans!). They grow and multiply by secretly using the cells, energy or food they've eaten.

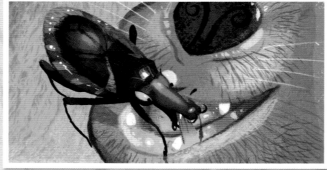

THE KISSING BUG

Far from sweet, this bug climbs on a dog's face or lips and sucks out their blood. As it's doing this, it poops out hundreds of *Trypanosoma cruzi* parasites, which go into the dog's blood. The parasite enters the dog's cells and multiplies, which can make the cells burst, before causing the dog to have a heart attack.

TAPEWORMS

Tapeworms lay their eggs in poop and dirt. Sheep eat that poop and dirt, along with grass. Once inside a sheep, the larvae (baby tapeworms) latch on to the wall of its intestines and grow longer and longer, feeding off all the blood and tasty treats that pass through its new home.

A tapeworm can grow up to 6 metres long inside the intestines!

GUINEA WORM

In Africa, there's the Guinea worm parasite. It grows inside a dog's stomach before forming a painful blister on the dog's skin. When the dog steps into a river or lake, the worm pops its head out and squirts Guinea worm larvae into the water... where they can be eaten by humans!

VAMPIRE LOUSE

Cymothoa exigua is a creepy, crab-like louse that can sneak inside fish. It then sucks up the fish's blood through the fish's tongue. As the louse grows, less blood reaches the fish's tongue and it eventually drops off. The louse then acts as a new tongue for the fish!

ZOMBIE MICE

There's a parasite that can make mice lose their fear of cats, it's called *Toxoplasma Gondii*. This makes a mouse walk right up to a cat, where it can be eaten. This is the parasite's cunning plan: *Toxoplasma Gondii* can only multiply inside the warm, cosy guts of cats.